THE JOY OF RESURRECTION

Devotionals written and edited by

Beverly Courrege

Photographs by

David and Stephanie Edmonson

A
JANET
THOMA
BOOK

THOMAS NELSON PUBLISHERS
Nashville

Published in Nashville, Tennessee, by Thomas Nelson, Inc.

Unless otherwise noted, Scripture quotations are from THE NEW KING JAMES VERSION. Copyright © 1979, 1980, 1982 Thomas Nelson, Inc., Publishers.

Scripture quotations marked NIV are from the HOLY BIBLE: NEW INTERNATIONAL VERSION®. Copyright © 1973, 1978, 1984 by International Bible Society. Used by permission of Zondervan Publishing House. All rights reserved.

Library of Congress Cataloging-in-Publication Data

Courrege, Beverly.
    The joy of resurrection : devotionals / written and edited by Beverly Courrege; photographs by David and Stephanie Edmonson.
        p. cm.
    ISBN 0–7852–6932–0
    1. Devotional literature, English. I. Title.
BV4832.2 .C668 2000
242—dc21
                                                                        99-05767
                                                                        CIP

Printed in the United States of America

2 3 4 5 6 7 8 9 10 QPK 09 08 07 06 05 04 03 02 01 00

Uncommon Virtue

A tribute
in loving memory of
Donald R. Block
Born: November 22, 1968
Born Again: July 15, 1997
Living Now in the Womb of Eternity Since
January 20, 1999

Contents

Acknowledgments

SPECIAL THANKS to David and Stephanie Edmonson for sharing this inspiring collection of photographs with me and the readers of this book.

Thank you, too, to the list of beloved authors and others whose words indeed add to the reader's joy of resurrection.

And always, blessings to Janet Thoma and everyone at Thomas Nelson. Thank you for your confidence in me and for allowing me the joy of yet another testimony to the glory of God, especially *The Joy of Resurrection!*

Introduction

THE PSALMIST WROTE, *"Be still, and know that I am God"* (Psalm 46:10). When I stand in the midst of God's creation and reflect on the detail and majesty of His hand in everything around me, I am always awed that His gift of the earth's beauty is my *present* salvation. This beauty is but a glimpse of what will come when I am resurrected with my Lord in eternity.

Do you have this assurance? Can you *be still and know* that He is Your God? Having this assurance, do you often take time to *be still* with Him?

Photographers David and Stephanie Edmonson capture these moments of *stillness* in God's presence on the edge of a seashore, standing on mountains, surrounded by an aspen forest, or gazing at flickering candlelight with beautiful images that will move you to reflect on who God is and who you are because of what He did for you and me.

It is my hope that through this book of inspiring devotions from many of your favorite authors, along with this special collection of David and Stephanie Edmonson's photography, you will seek time to *be still* and experience THE JOY OF RESURRECTION.

The Incarnation Is a Thing Too Wonderful

BY ELISABETH ELLIOT

And without controversy great is the mystery of godliness:

God was manifested in the flesh,

Justified in the Spirit,

Seen by angels,

Preached among the Gentiles,

Believed on in the world,

Received up in glory.

1 Timothy 3:16 NKJV

SOME THINGS are simply too wonderful for explanation—the navigational system of the Arctic tern, for example. How does it find its way over twelve thousand miles of ocean from its nesting grounds in the Arctic to its wintering grounds in the Antarctic! Ornithologists have conducted all sorts of tests without finding the answer. *Instinct* is the best they can offer—no explanation at all, merely a way of saying that they really have no idea. A Laysan albatross was once released 3,200 miles from its nest in the Midway Islands. It was back home in ten days.

The migration of birds is a thing too wonderful.

When the angel Gabriel told Mary, "You will be with child and give birth to a son," she had a simple question about the natural: How can this be, since I am a virgin?!

The answer had to do not with the natural but with something far more mysterious than the tern's navigation—something, in fact, entirely supernatural: "The Holy Spirit will come upon you, and the Most High will overshadow you" (Luke 1:35, NIV). That was too wonderful, and Mary was silent. She had no question about the supernatural. She was satisfied with God's answer.

The truth about the Incarnation is a thing too wonderful for us. Who can fathom what really took place first in a virgin's womb in Nazareth and then in a stable in Bethlehem? . . .

Mary's acceptance of the angel's answer to her innocent question was immediate, though she could not imagine the intricacies and mysteries of its working in her young virgin body. She surrendered herself utterly to God in trust and obedience.

Do you *understand* what is going on in the invisible realm of your life with God? Do you *see* how the visible things relate to the hidden Plan and Purpose? Probably not. As my second husband, Addison Leitch, used to say, "You can't unscrew the Inscrutable." But you do see at least one thing, maybe a very little thing, that He wants to do. "Now what I am commanding you today is not too difficult [other translations say "too hard," "too wonderful"] for you or beyond your reach. It is up to heaven . . . nor is it beyond the sea . . . no, the word is very near you; it is in your mouth and in your heart so you may obey it" (Deuteronomy 30:11-14, NIV).

Let it suffice you, as it sufficed Mary, to know that God knows. If it's time to work, get on with your job. If it's time to go to bed, go to sleep in peace. Let the Lord of the universe do the worrying.[1]

—From *Keep a Quiet Heart*

GOD INCARNATE IN CHRIST

He is the image of the invisible God, the firstborn over all creation. For by Him all things were created that are in heaven and that are on earth, visible and invisible, whether thrones or dominions or principalities or powers. All things were created through Him and for Him. And He is before all things, and in Him all things consist.

Colossians 1:15-17 NKJV

The Humility of Christ

BY ANDREW MURRAY

Jesus, knowing that the Father had given all things into His hands, and that He had come from God and was going to God, rose from supper and laid aside His garments, took a towel and girded Himself. After that, He poured water into a basin and began to wash the disciples' feet, and to wipe them with the towel with which He was girded. Then He came to Simon Peter. And Peter said to Him, "Lord, are You washing my feet?" Jesus answered and said to him, "What I am doing you do not understand now, but you will know after this." Peter said to Him, "You shall never wash my feet!" Jesus answered him, "If I do not wash you, you have no part with Me."

John 13:3–8 NKJV

HUMILITY is the salvation that Christ brings. That is our first thought. We often have very vague—I might also say visionary—ideas of what Christ is. We love the person of Christ, but that which makes up Christ, which actually constitutes Him as the Christ, we do not know or love. If we love Christ above everything, we must love humility above everything, for humility is the very essence of His life and glory and the salvation He brings. Just think of it. Where did it begin? Is there humility in heaven? You know there is, for they cast their crowns before the throne of God and the Lamb. But, is there humility on the throne of God? Yes, what was it but heavenly humility that made Jesus on the throne willing to say: "I will go down to be a servant, and to die for man. I will go and live as the meek and lowly Lamb of God"?

Jesus brought humility from heaven to us. It was humility that brought Him to earth, or He would have never come. In accordance with this, just as Christ became a man in this divine humility, so His whole life was marked by it. He might have chosen another form in which to appear. He might have come in the form of a king, but He chose the form of a servant. He said: "The Son of Man came not to be ministered unto, but to minister, and to give His life a ransom for many" (Matthew 20:28). And you know, in the last night, He took the place of a slave, girded Himself with a towel, and went to wash the feet of Peter and the other disciples.

Beloved, the life of Jesus upon the earth was a life of the deepest humility. It was this which gave His life its worth and beauty in God's sight. And then, His death—possibly you haven't thought of it much in this connection—but His death was an exhibition of unparalleled humility. "He humbled Himself, and became obedient unto death, even the death of the cross." My Lord Jesus Christ occupied a low place during His time on earth. He took a very low place when He began to wash the disciples' feet. But, when He went to Calvary, He took the lowest place there was to be found in the universe of God, the very lowest. He let sin, the curse of sin, and the wrath of God cover Him. He took the place of a guilty sinner, that He might bear our load, that He might serve us in saving us from our wretchedness, that He might, by His precious blood, win deliverance for us, that He might, by that blood, wash us from our stain and our guilt.[2]

—From *The Master's Indwelling*

Have you let go of your pride? Do you have a servant's heart?

CHRIST: HUMBLED AND EXALTED

Let this mind be in you which was also in Christ Jesus, who, being in the form of God, did not consider it robbery to be equal with God, but made Himself of no reputation, taking the form of a bondservant, and coming in the likeness of men. And being found in appearance as a man, He humbled Himself and became obedient to the point of death, even the death of the cross. Therefore God also has highly exalted Him and given Him the name which is above every name, that at the name of Jesus every knee should bow, of those in heaven, and of those on earth, and of those under the earth, and that every tongue should confess that Jesus Christ is Lord, to the glory of God the Father.

Philippians 2:5–11 NKJV

The Last Supper

Then came the Day of Unleavened Bread, when the Passover must be killed. And He sent Peter and John, saying, "Go and prepare the Passover for us, that we may eat." So they said to Him, "Where do You want us to prepare?" And He said to them, "Behold, when you have entered the city, a man will meet you carrying a pitcher of water; follow him into the house which he enters. Then you shall say to the master of the house, 'The Teacher says to you, "Where is the guest room where I may eat the Passover with My disciples?"' Then he will show you a large, furnished upper room; there make ready." So they went and found it just as He had said to them, and they prepared the Passover.

Luke 22:7–13 NKJV

I OFTEN MENTION my daughter's friend Lindsay because, as our neighbor, she was in our lives nearly every day for sixteen years. I experienced life through her eyes almost as often as through the eyes of my daughter, J. J.

One day Lindsay and J. J. were at my kitchen table discussing recent events, and Lindsay began telling J. J. about the death of her uncle that week. Lindsay said that her uncle had just eaten dinner at a café and had died while walking across the street to his car. She related the story so matter-of-factly that at first I was concerned she might not comprehend the word *died.* I didn't interrupt her narrative, however. I'm glad I didn't.

She continued: "I wonder what he ate for his last supper? I know what I'd like to eat for *my* last supper. Tacos!" And that was that.

I have often thought about Lindsay's reference to her last supper and have asked myself, *If I knew it was to be my last supper, what would I eat, where would I eat, with whom would I eat my last supper, and would I choose to serve or be served?*

I wonder when Jesus made the arrangements with the owner of the upper room for the last meal with His disciples. The accounts of this arrangement in Matthew and Mark tell us that the room was already prepared.

What a night that must have been. Jesus was surrounded by His best friends, and He knew that Satan would enter Judas and be right in the room with all of them (John 13:27). Picture in your mind Jesus having washed Judas' feet, knowing Judas' heart had already been snatched by Satan. Satan had also asked Jesus for Peter, too, to "sift him as wheat" (Luke 22:31). Peter was nestled safely against Jesus' chest when Satan entered Judas—this, to me, was a picture of Christ's love and protection, even though He knew that for a time Peter, too, would deny Him.

If you knew it would be your last supper, would you comfort your friends or seek comfort? Would you prepare them for what was to come or seek their sympathy? Would you have the energy to resolve conflict? Would you serve your friends and family, or would you feel entitled to be served?

When we observe Christ's last supper, let's not only remember that the bread and cup represent His broken body and His poured-out blood. Let us also remember Jesus' example of comforting, calming, and serving as He faced death.

Thirst for the Living God

As the deer pants for the
    water brooks,
So pants my soul for You,
    O God.
My soul thirsts for God, for the
    living God.
When shall I come and
    appear before God?

Psalm 42:1–2 NKJV

The Plan

BY MAX LUCADO

For whom He foreknew, He also predestined to be conformed to the image of His Son, that He might be the firstborn among many brethren.

Romans 8:29 NKJV

READ THIS QUOTE from the first sermon ever preached about the cross [Acts 2:22–23 NIV] and see if you can find the revealing phrase.

> Men of Israel, listen to this: Jesus of Nazareth was a man accredited by God to you by miracles, wonders and signs, which God did among you through him, as you yourselves know. This man was handed over to you by God's set purpose and foreknowledge; and you, with the help of wicked men, put him to death by nailing him to the cross.

Did you see it? It's the solemn phrase in the paragraph. It's the statement that rings of courage, the one with roots that extend back to eternity. It is the phrase which, perhaps as much as any in the Bible, describes the real price God paid to adopt you.

Which phrase? "God's set purpose and foreknowledge." The *Revised Standard Version* calls it "the definite plan and foreknowledge of God." *Today's English Version* translates the phrase "In accordance with his own plan."

15

What does that mean? It means Jesus planned His own sacrifice.

It means Jesus intentionally planted the tree from which His cross would be carved.

It means He willingly placed the iron ore in the heart of the earth from which nails would be cast.

It means He voluntarily placed His Judas in the womb of a woman.

It means Christ was the one who set in motion the political machinery that would send Pilate to Jerusalem.

And it means He didn't have to do it—but He did.

Jesus was born crucified.[3]

—From *God Came Near*

Jesus included you in *His* plan. Have you included Jesus in *your* plans?

Jesus Reveals the Plan

"And I, if I am lifted up from the earth, will draw all peoples to Myself."
This He said, signifying by what death He would die.

John 12:32–33 NKJV

How Long Is Forever?

*Having been born again, not of corruptible seed but incorruptible, through the word
of God which lives and abides forever, because*
    "All flesh is as grass,
    And all the glory of man as the flower of the grass.
    The grass withers,
    And its flower falls away,
    But the word of the LORD endures forever."

1 Peter 1:23–25 NKJV

FOREVER IS a long time! Genesis was probably penned about fifteen hundred years before Christ, and we still have those same words some thirty-five hundred years later. When I think of all the Christians who have read the same Scriptures—not only Christians today but also Christians throughout the ages—then I realize that my mind cannot grasp what *forever* means as it relates to the Word of God.

Even though seasons of grass have withered in the same fields, and thousands of generations of men have ceased to breathe on this earth, God, through His Word, has forever breathed eternal life—forever life—into those who believe.

On October 5, 1958, when I was ten years old, I walked down the aisle to profess my faith and received my first Bible. Even then I knew that the Bible is a treasure. I was fascinated with the colorful illustrations of stories I had heard each week in Sunday school. The inscription at the beginning of the New Testament awed me:

"With all the words recorded therein as having been spoken by Our Lord printed in red."

I probably didn't understand those words at the time, but I remember that I didn't want to travel on vacations without bringing my Bible. On one trip with my family, I left my Bible open to a picture in the Old Testament of Moses destroying the stone tablets. Since our car didn't have air-conditioning, we left the windows down. While we were out of the car, it began to rain. Rain splattered the pages of my open Bible. When I came back to the car and saw my Bible, I almost splattered the pages even more with my tears. My dad assured me that the pages would be fine, once they dried out.

While I was writing this story, I got out that Bible and turned to those water-soaked pages. My dad had been right—the pages had dried out. God's eternal Word has endured for forty years for me. How long is *forever* for you?

THE TIMELESS EXISTENCE OF GOD

"I am the Alpha and the Omega,

the Beginning and the End,"

says the Lord,

"who is and who was

and who is to come,

the Almighty."

Revelation 1:8 NKJV

Vessels

BY RUTH BELL GRAHAM

Now when evening came, His disciples went down to the sea, got into the boat, and went . . . toward Capernaum . . . Then the sea arose because a great wind was blowing . . . they saw Jesus walking on the sea and drawing near the boat; and they were afraid. But He said to them, "It is I; do not be afraid."

John 6:16–20 NKJV

What of the folk back home that day the sudden storm swept Galilee? Knowing the violence of the storms, the smallness of the craft, did they abandon themselves to grief, or say, "The one who sails with him is He who made the storm-filled universe, the height, the depth, the everywhere; the storm is fierce, the craft is small, but He is there!"?[4]

—From *Sitting by My Laughing Fire*

WHEN THE WAVES are too high, the seas are rolling, and the boat is rocking on the verge of sinking, do others see panic or peace in us? Is our vessel seaworthy—not just for sailing along a glassy sea but also for the sudden storms, twenty-foot swells, and gale-force winds?

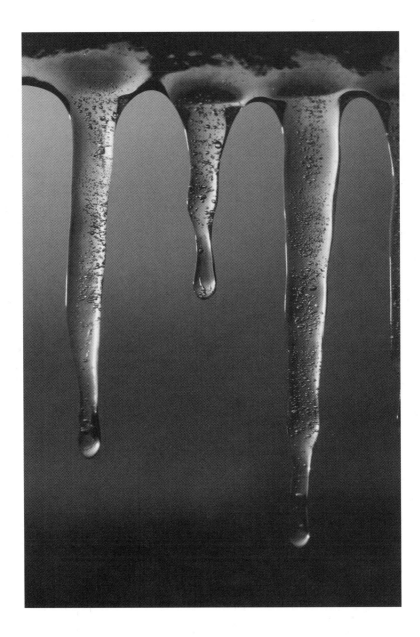

Change

BY A.W. TOZER

So teach us to number our days,
That we may gain a heart of wisdom.

Psalm 90:12 NKJV

What a broad world to roam in, what a sea to swim in is the God and Father of our Lord Jesus Christ. He is eternal. He antedates time and is wholly independent of it. Time began in Him and will end with Him. To it He pays no tribute and from it He suffers no change. He is immutable. He has never changed and can never change in any smallest measure. To change, He would need to go from better to worse or from worse to better. He cannot do either, for being perfect, He cannot become more perfect, and if He were to become less perfect, He would be less than God.[5]

—From *The Pursuit of God*

GOD DOES not change. He does allow us to change, however, so that we might become more like Him. Let us prayerfully number each new day; only then will we change from worse to better.

25

Solitude

BY ANNE MORROW LINDBERGH

And He said to them, "Come aside by yourselves to a deserted place and rest a while."

Mark 6:31 NKJV

FOR A FULL DAY and two nights I have been alone. I lay on the beach under the stars at night alone. I made my breakfast alone. Alone I watched the gulls at the end of the pier, dip and wheel and dive for the scraps I threw them. A morning's work at my desk, and then, a late picnic lunch alone on the beach.

And it seemed to me, separated from my own species, that I was nearer to others: the shy willet, nesting in the tide-wash behind me; the sandpiper, running in little frightened steps down the shining beach rim ahead of me; the slowly flapping pelicans over my head, coasting down wind; the old gull, hunched up, grouchy, surveying the horizon. I felt an impersonal kinship with them and a joy in that kinship. Beauty of earth and sea and air meant more to me. I was in harmony with it, melted into the universe, lost in it, as one is lost in a canticle of praise, swelling from an unknown crowd in a cathedral. "Praise ye the Lord, all ye fishes of the sea—all ye birds of the air—all ye children of men—Praise ye the Lord!"

Yes, I felt closer to my fellow man too, even in my solitude. For it is not physical solitude that actually separates one from other men, not physical isolation, but spiritual isolation. It is not the desert island nor the stony wilderness that cuts you from the people you love. It is the wilderness in the mind, the desert wastes through which one wanders lost and is a stranger. When one is a stranger to oneself, then one is estranged from others too. If one is out of touch with oneself, then one cannot touch others. How often in a large city, shaking hands with my friends, I have felt the wilderness stretching between us. Both of us were wandering in arid wastes, having lost the springs that nourished us—or having found them dry.

Only when one is connected to one's own core is one connected to others, I am beginning to discover. And, for me, the core, the inner spring, can best be refound through solitude.[6]

—From *Gift from the Sea*

SOLITUDE WITH GOD

Your words were found, and I
    ate them,
And Your word was to me the
    joy and rejoicing of my heart;
For I am called by Your name,
O Lord God of hosts.

Jeremiah 15:16 NKJV

Be still, and know that
I am God.

Psalm 46:10 NKJV

Rising Waters

God understands its way,

And He knows its place.

For He looks to the ends of the earth,

And sees under the whole heavens,

To establish a weight for the wind,

And apportion the waters by measure.

Job 28:23–27 NKJV

ONE JULY MORNING I awoke to a news report that campers from a Dallas-area church had been caught in a flash flood along the Guadalupe River while trying to evacuate to higher ground. Rushing water swept forty-three teenagers and adults downriver. Only thirty-three people survived. Two teenage victims lost their lives while saving other children.

Why did this tragedy happen? That is one of our eternal questions.

God chose the path for the flowing waters, and He knew who lay in that path's course. As the Scripture says, He "apportions the waters by measure."

Even though those young lives were tragically lost, there is still hope. I believe that those victims were not lost. Instead they are in His presence, "where their feet are on *the rock*, and the waters cannot overwhelm them"— resurrected with our Lord!

The Lighthouse

BY CORD COURREGE

The LORD is my light and my salvation;
Whom shall I fear?

Psalm 27:1 NKJV

A lighthouse stands alone.
Its greatness towers over tormenting waters and rocks of destructive power.
Its beacon shines through black night to each oncoming vessel.
The Lord is the lighthouse in the life of each Christian.

The Christian travels like a ship through waves of trials and rocks of tribulations.
The beacon of light is the Word of God, directing each ship to a worthier, safer place.

Currents from raging waters tempt each ship to turn away
from the light and travel recklessly
through the blackness of night toward ultimate destruction.

This temptation can only be overcome by putting complete faith in the Lord's beacon,
and by allowing Him to be the Captain of one's soul.[7]

Pearls

A man has joy by the answer of his mouth,

   And a word spoken in due season, how good it is!

Proverbs 15:23 NKJV

I HAVE ALWAYS loved to dress up. As a teenager in the early 1960s, I often wore a suit, heels, and pearls to church.

I was always the first one to arrive at Sunday school and the last one to leave. One Sunday morning I was sitting at the piano, waiting for my friends to show up. My band director's beautiful wife came up to me. She had never before spoken to me one-on-one, but that morning she noticed me sitting alone.

"Good morning, Beverly. You're here early."

I only smiled. Adults rarely spoke to me, so I wasn't sure what to say.

She went on, "You have a beautiful smile. It lights up your eyes. And you're dressed so 'smart' today. I like your choice of pearls. You should always wear pearls. They reflect your warmth and charm and smooth complexion."

Smooth complexion? I thought. *Didn't I just cover up some zits before I left the house?*

"They are as feminine and perfect as you are. They suit you. Yes, you should always wear pearls."

That was the end of our "conversation." She walked away. I never saw or spoke with her again—until she was diagnosed with cancer, and my fellow band members and I filed past her hospital bed. I remember thinking that she was so young. She

35

didn't have any gray hair or wrinkles, and her nails were long and impeccably man-icured. She was very feminine.

She is what I felt *feminine* should be, and she had told me *I* was feminine. I didn't understand then that she was dying.

When she died, I remembered what she had said the only time she ever spoke to me. Now every time I wear pearls, I think of her. That happened an eternity ago. Did her words have eternal value?

My aunt had given me the pearls that I had worn that Sunday morning. I still have them, and my daughter also wore them when she was in her early teens. I don't know whether the pearls are real, but they are precious to me.

When I see a pearl, I remember a godly woman who took the time to speak to an impressionable, insecure teen and to encourage me to see positive traits in my appearance and character. Thank you, Mrs. Smith, for giving to the Lord with your words of beauty and life.

What words of eternal value will you leave for others to remember?

GRATITUDE FOR GOD'S GOODNESS

I remember the days of old;

I meditate on all Your works;

I muse on the work of Your hands.

I spread out my hands to You;

My soul longs for You like a thirsty land.

Psalm 143:5–6 NKJV

Joy in Abiding

I am the true vine, and My Father is the vinedresser . . . Abide in Me, and I in you. As the branch cannot bear fruit of itself, unless it abides in the vine, neither can you unless you abide in Me. I am the vine, you are the branches. He who abides in Me, and I in him, bears much fruit; for without Me you can do nothing.

John 15:4–5 NKJV

THE FLOWER we know as cyclamen, sometimes called "Solomon's crown," may have been around in biblical times. It may be one of the flowers referred to in the "lilies of the field" passage (Matt. 6:28). The Gospels sometimes recount that Jesus and His disciples were in a garden. I imagine they found beauty, quiet, and rest there. Did the disciples think of Christ's words about the lilies, how "they toil not"? When I see a single-stemmed plant with multiple flowers, I think of Christ's lilies of the field and His teaching on abiding in Him (John 15).

Christians are the many flowers from one common stem, Christ. We died with Him, were buried with Him, and are **raised** with Him! Just as the plants in our gardens bloom more abundantly when we prune and feed them, we also yield the fruit God desires when He prunes and tends us.

Our heavenly Father shapes us. We cannot do it ourselves. We should abide in Him like the lilies of the field, neither toiling nor spinning. God began the work in us, and He will complete it. The joy in abiding is always ours. Our joy is multiplied when we bring others to be transformed and added to His beautiful lilies of His field.

A Rippling Tide

*Thus says the L*ORD*, your Redeemer,*
The Holy One of Israel:
*"I am the L*ORD*, your God,*
Who teaches you to profit,
Who leads you by the way you should go.
Oh, that you heeded My commandments!
Then your peace would have been like a river,
And your righteousness like the waves of the sea."

Isaiah 48:17–18 NKJV

ONE DESCRIPTION of the word *rippling* is that of water running over and slightly agitating a rough, pebbly surface. The righteousness of Christians is like the waves of the sea. When we take a stand for higher values in our world, there is a rippling effect. Think of worldly values as the rough pebbles and Christians' righteousness as the agitators.

Have you ever stood at the water's edge and watched the rocks or seashells as the tide goes in and out? Sometimes the rocks are displaced. Sometimes the rocks reappear exactly where you are watching. And then sometimes the rocks vanish.

Christians are a similar catalyst for change in a world of aggregate pebbles that sometimes become gigantic boulders. And just as the coastlines and waterways are sometimes mired in toxic sludge, actually changing lives can be as tedious as removing the sludge to expose the muck and mire.

Only Christ can cause the "rippling" of His righteousness in this rocky world. First Corinthians 4:1-5 (NKJV) emphasizes this:

> Let a man so consider us, as servants of Christ and stewards of the mysteries of God. Moreover it is required in stewards that one be found faithful. But with me it is a very small thing that I should be judged by you or by a human court. In fact, I do not even judge myself. For I know of nothing against myself, yet I am not justified by this; but He who judges me is the Lord. Therefore judge nothing before the time, until the Lord comes, who will both bring to light the hidden things of darkness and reveal the counsels of the hearts. Then each one's praise will come from God.

Do we as Christians want to be instruments of change, to improve our world? If so, we cannot judge. We must be found faithful. That faithfulness—and Christ in us—causes the rippling of righteousness that can not only remove rocks and boulders but can also move mountains!

LEAD A CONSISTENT LIFE

Who is wise and understanding among you?
Let him show by good conduct that his works are done
in the meekness of wisdom.

James 3:13 NKJV

Therefore be imitators of God as dear children. And
walk in love, as Christ also has loved us and given
Himself for us, an offering and a sacrifice to God for a
sweet-smelling aroma.

Ephesians 5:1–2 NKJV

See then that you walk circumspectly, not as fools
but as wise, redeeming the time, because the days are evil.

Ephesians 5:15–16 NKJV

Echoes of Mercy

My soul still remembers
And sinks within me.
This I recall to my mind,
Therefore I have hope.
Through the LORD's mercies we are not consumed,
Because His compassions fail not.
They are new every morning;
Great is Your faithfulness.
"The LORD is my portion," says my soul,
"Therefore I hope in Him!"

Lamentations 3:20-24 NKJV

THERE ARE ADVANTAGES to being a slow skier. I prefer to think of myself as a *controlled* skier. Since I didn't learn to ski until I was thirty-eight, you can understand why my only goal on the slopes is not to fall!

Our family and friends like to be first in the lift lines each morning so they can have the luxury of being the first ones down the new powder that has fallen overnight—or that may still be falling in subzero temperatures. Have you gotten the message that snow skiing is *not* my sport of choice?

However, I allow myself to be awakened while it is still dark, to be bundled in five layers of clothing, and literally pulled to our position in the lift line so we have the advantage of first *run*. Before he and our friends have finished putting on their skis, my husband usually positions me at the front so I'll be ready to go down first. Over the years I have accepted this rather solicitous treatment as a type of TLC rather than seeing it as their annoyance that I might not keep up with the pack.

I would be content to ride the lift up and down the mountain all day, never getting off, but that is not allowed. In fact, strategically placed signs near the summit state quite clearly: Keep your tips up while *leaving* the lift. You *must* get off!

Then we are at the top. Here is where the advantage of being slowest comes in. Everyone agrees that I should take off first. The first time they insisted I be first, I am sure they were concerned for me, just in case I fell. As the years progressed and I found my comfort zone, they were as concerned about passing me and leaving me behind as they were afraid that I would fall. So now, without fail, I am always "allowed" to go first.

I look out over the horizon with mixed emotions, sometimes closing my eyes to ward off an attack of vertigo. But once I have pushed myself off and have found my "zone," peace, contentment, and well-being wash over me. I ski down the slope alone with my thoughts, and often those thoughts are of God in all His majesty. I refuse to believe that a skier would dare profess to be an atheist. The evidence of a Hand greater than ours is so obvious!

When I'm out in front, nothing is ahead of me but wide-open runs lined by snow-covered trees. My breath inside my ski mask warms my face. It is so quiet. I come to a level expanse on the slope, and, not stopping, I close my eyes, but only for a few seconds!

Did you know there are blind skiers? What I experience for a few seconds is what they experience all the time. Their other senses are so heightened that the distractions of their performance and of other skiers are not important. They can simply ski and feel God's presence.

Fanny Crosby, a hymn writer and poet, was blind, but she probably never skied. In 1864 at the age of forty-four, she began writing hymns. Until her death in 1915 at the age of ninety-five, historians estimate she wrote between fifty-five hundred and nine thousand hymns. The exact number eludes us because she modestly wrote under pseudonyms to escape the spotlight on herself. Rare individual, indeed! One of her hymns, "Blessed Assurance," contains the phrase "echoes of mercy, whispers of love." Fanny had a long life of echoes and whispers, yet she wrote of her blessings in spite of being blind.

"Echoes of mercy" and "whispers of love" best describe the early morning, quiet, first run in the snow in the presence of God. His breeze blows across my face, kissing my brow. His sun warms my skin. His wind in the trees whispers my name. When I close my eyes, I hear echoes of His mercies for me—mercies that are new each morning.

Close your eyes and listen to His whispers of love and the echoes of all the mercies He has given you. Sometimes it takes closing our eyes to focus on God's love and His mercies. And, yes, sometimes, going slowly has its advantages.

Boundaries

BY CORD COURREGE

Jesus said to him, "I am the way, the truth, and the life.
No one comes to the Father except through Me."

John 14:6 NKJV

Boundaries that people have created
have separated them since the beginning of time.
With every fence we build, divisions are made.
The Word of God is the only
standard that should determine
our values.
The Lord knows no boundaries.
His heart is vaster than
anything His children know.
His open arms of never-ending love
and understanding are the only limits He supplies.
Without a relationship with God,
the boundaries we create
build walls against His ultimate plan of everlasting life.[8]

Activating God's Power

BY RUTH MYERS

The voice of one crying in the wilderness:
"Prepare the way of the LORD;
Make straight in the desert
A highway for our God.
Every valley shall be exalted
And every mountain and hill brought low;
The crooked places shall be made straight
And the rough places smooth."

Isaiah 40:3–4 NKJV

AS YOU PRAY and praise the Lord, you free God to reveal His power as well as His Presence. Prayer has been called the "slender nerve that moves the mighty hand of God" (source unknown). Any form of sincere, believing prayer directs God's power into our lives and situations, but this is especially true of prayer blended with praise.

Your praise and thanksgiving can help form a highway—a smooth, level road—on which the Lord can ride forth unhindered to deliver and bless.[9]

—From *31 Days of Praise*

The Roar

BY MAX LUCADO

So Jesus said to them again, "Peace to you! As the Father has sent Me, I also send you."

John 20:21 NKJV

THE DOOR is locked. Deadbolted. Maybe even a chair under the doorknob. Inside sit ten knee-knocking itinerants who are astraddle the fence between faith and fear.

As you look around the room, you wouldn't take them for a bunch who are about to put the kettle of history on high boil. Uneducated. Confused. Calloused hands. Heavy accents. Few social graces. Limited knowledge of the world. No money. Undefined leadership. And on and on.

No, as you look at this motley crew, you wouldn't wager too many paychecks on their future. But something happens to a man when he witnesses someone who has risen from the dead. Something stirs within the soul of a man who has stood within inches of God. Something stirs that is hotter than gold fever and more permanent than passion.

It all started with the stammering, stuttering men. Though the door was locked, He still stood in their midst. "As the Father has sent me, I am sending you."

And send them He did. Ports. Courtyards. Boats. Synagogues. Prisons. Palaces. They went everywhere. Their message of the Nazarene dominoed across the civilized world. They were an infectious fever. They were a moving organism. They refused to be stopped. Uneducated drifters who shook history like a housewife shakes a rug.

My, wouldn't it be great to see it happen again?

Many say it's impossible. The world is too hard. Too secular. Too post-Christian. "This is the age of information, not regeneration." So we deadbolt the door for fear of the world.

And as a result, the world goes largely untouched and untaught. Over half of the world has yet to hear the story of the Messiah, much less study it. The few believers who do go out often come home weary and wounded, numbed at the odds and frustrated at the needs.

What would it take to light the fire again? Somehow, those fellows in the upper room did it. They did it without dragging their feet or making excuses. For them it was rather obvious. "All I know is that He was dead and now He is alive."

Something happens to a man when he stands within inches of the Judaean Lion. Something happens when he hears the roar, when he touches the golden mane. Something happens when he gets so close he can feel the Lion's breath. Maybe we could all use a return visit. Maybe we all need to witness His majesty and sigh at His victory. Maybe we need to hear our own commission again. "Will you tell them?" Jesus challenged. "Will you tell them that I came back . . . and that I am coming back again?"

"We will," they nodded. And they did.

Will you?[10]

—From *No Wonder They Call Him the Savior*

The Calling of the Saved

. . . who has saved us and called us to a holy calling,
not according to our works, but according to His own purpose and grace
which was given to us in Christ Jesus before time began,
but has now been revealed by the appearing of our Savior Jesus Christ . . .

2 Timothy 1:9–10 NKJV

Preach the word! Be ready in season and out of season.
Convince, rebuke, exhort, with all longsuffering and teaching.

2 Timothy 4:2 NKJV

I, therefore . . . beseech you to walk worthy of the calling with which you were called, with all lowliness and gentleness, with longsuffering, bearing with one another in love, endeavoring to keep the unity of the Spirit in the bond of peace.

Ephesians 4:1–3 NKJV

Co-Creator of the New Nature

When He had been baptized, Jesus came up immediately from the water; and behold, the heavens were opened up to Him, and He saw the Spirit of God descending like a dove and alighting upon Him. And suddenly a voice came from heaven, saying, "This is My beloved Son, in whom I am well pleased."

Matthew 3:16–17 NKJV

He is co-Creator of the new nature.

Our Lord's birth by the Spirit is a type of our new birth or rebirth. It is "that which is born of the Spirit" (John 3:6); "born . . . of God" (3:3); "through the Spirit . . . being born again"(1 Pet. 1:22, 23); "a new creation" (2 Cor. 5:17).

The notable difference between the creation of our Lord's physical nature and the creation of our spiritual nature by the same Spirit can be expressed this way: At the Virgin Birth of Christ there was added to His already existing divine nature a human nature while at our rebirth the Spirit adds a divine nature to an already existing human nature.

Regeneration does not make a sinner a better man, but brings in a new man. By faith the believing one is made a partaker of the divine nature.[11]

—From *The Holy Spirit of God*

WHEN MY DAUGHTER J. J. and her friend Lindsay were about six years old, they had a discussion about ghosts. Lindsay asked J. J. if she believed in ghosts. J. J. replied, "Maybe, but they are different than the Holy Ghost."

They were having this discussion because it was the week of Halloween when, unfortunately, ghostly apparitions are prevalent on TV, in some classrooms, and in retail stores. My husband and I had taught our children, from the time we felt they could understand, how Halloween began and that we chose to celebrate this "fall festival" in a church environment.

I was all ears because even though J. J. had been in church since she was a baby, I had no idea she had heard about the Holy Spirit, much less the name Holy Ghost.

J. J. went on to explain to Lindsay, "Even if there are really ghosts, they are not like the Holy Ghost because they are all different, and the Holy Ghost is the same all the time." She then said, "There might be a ghost in a room, but the Holy Ghost is everywhere all the time. And the Holy Ghost won't scare you. He's a good ghost."

Perhaps you are wondering why I feel this conversation has merit. If, at the age of six, my daughter didn't quite have the total grasp of the *person* of the Holy Spirit, she had a grasp on the *nature* of the Holy Spirit. I think it is significant, too, that we should be as innocent as children and accept that God is real and that He is good. Prayerfully, as an individual matures in the Lord, the significance of that goodness is a moment-by-moment reality. We are taught in the Scriptures that "divine nature" is within us and is, as my daughter said, "good."

Acknowledging the "divine nature" of the Holy Spirit within us moment by moment separates us from that old human nature. Perhaps you might even say it makes us "good."

My daughter is now twenty-two years old and understands the work of the Holy Spirit in her life. I often lovingly refer to her "as my personal Holy Spirit" when she lets me know that I've missed the mark.

> That good thing which was committed to you, keep by the Holy Spirit who dwells in us.
>
> 2 Timothy 1:14 NKJV

> In Him we have also obtained an inheritance . . .
> in Him you also trusted, after you heard the word of truth, the gospel of your salvation; in whom also, having believed, you were sealed with the Holy Spirit of promise, who is the guarantee of our inheritance.
>
> Ephesians 1:11, 13–14 NKJV

Christians Among Us

You are the light of the world. A city that is set on a hill cannot be hidden. Nor do they light a lamp and put it under a basket, but on a lampstand, and it gives light to all who are in the house. Let your light so shine before men, that they may see your good works and glorify your Father in heaven.

Matthew 5:14–16 NKJV

CHRISTIANS are among us, disguised as mothers, fathers, sisters, brothers, neighbors, coworkers, civic leaders, sons, and daughters. Can you recognize them? Perhaps you know someone who:

- puts others before themselves
- gives more than what is required
- always has a kind word
- serves rather than being served
- never gossips
- is a peacemaker
- cares for the aging
- is involved
- never lies
- honors his parents
- loves her neighbor
- is content whatever circumstance he is in
- has invited you to spend eternity with her

Do you know any of these people? Are you one of the Christians among us? Are you the light in the dark? Would we recognize you? Or have you disguised yourself too well as a "natural man"?

First Response

Though the fig tree may not blossom,
Nor fruit be on the vines;
Though the labor of the olive may fail,
And the fields yield no food;
Though the flock may be cut off from the fold,
And there be no herd in the stalls—
Yet I will rejoice in the LORD,
I will joy in the God of my salvation.
The LORD God is my strength;
He will make my feet like deer's feet,
And He will make me walk on my high hills.

Habakkuk 3:17–19 NKJV

OUR SON, Cord, is twenty-four and is an avid skier. Since the age of eight, he has been able to ski any terrain at breakneck speeds. Nevertheless, when he got lost on the mountain at age eleven, I panicked.

On that particular ski trip, our church group had taken shuttles from the lodge to the ski area. It took several shuttles to get everyone to the lifts. Our group always began the day together, even though we were at different levels of performance.

After our first leisurely run *en masse* down a gentle slope, we split up into smaller groups to allow each person to ski at peak performance. Cord and my husband, Boo, set out with the black-slopes group to hit every difficult course. I skied a gentle slope for most of the day.

At the end of the day, we all met at the bottom of the mountain to take a final run or depart for the lodge. The most advanced skiers didn't want to quit and urged others to take the last lift up and ski down one more time. By then each of us had a favorite course and didn't pay too much attention to everyone else's whereabouts. I thought Cord was with Boo, and Boo thought Cord was with me.

I finished the run and didn't see any of my friends at the shuttle. I decided they had already finished and gone back to the lodge, so I took the shuttle.

When we all got to the lodge, I saw some children, but Cord wasn't with them. Boo wasn't around either, so I assumed they had not gotten back yet. But just minutes later I saw Boo standing with other friends on the lodge grounds. I went over to him and asked, "Where's Cord?" He replied, "I thought he was with you."

By now the lifts were twenty minutes away and had closed for the day. Shuttles were still arriving, however, so I thought perhaps Cord would be on one of them. But he wasn't.

My mind screamed, *I have to do something!* The unthinkable was that Cord was still on the mountain by himself! In the winter, the sun sets early behind the mountains. It would be dark in less than an hour. I had to get back to the lifts.

A friend volunteered to drive me back up the mountain while Boo waited for Cord at the lodges. I am ashamed to say that prayer was not my first response to this crisis. Why is it that we let ourselves agonize in panic during a crisis? Instead of prayer being our first response, it is often our last resort.

Christ, on the other hand, prayed all the time. His attitude of prayer was as constant as breathing. He prayed during crises for His needs and the needs of others. He prayed in thanksgiving. He prayed in worship. He prayed for God's presence. Sometimes he prayed all night.

My friend Doak, who was driving me to the lifts, said, "Let's pray" the moment he turned the key to start the car. His words jolted me. I remember thinking, *I should have thought of that*, and just as quickly thinking, *I don't know what I should pray for.* Our minds do that sometimes in a crisis. Sometimes the most complete thought we can muster is *Help!* (also known as an S.O.S. prayer).

But Doak prayed aloud for the entire twenty-minute drive. Soft Christian music played on the radio. I closed my eyes and let the hymns and Doak's words wash over me. Immediately I felt God's presence—and the peace that had eluded me—wash over me.

When the car stopped, Doak said what I already felt: "Cord is okay. He's probably waiting for us."

I ran toward the lifts and a young ski-patroller smiled as she pointed me in the right direction. As I rounded the corner of the lift house, Cord ran toward me crying, but he was okay. When we embraced, he said, "I knew you would come, Mom."

Eleven-year-old Cord met his first "high place" that day. He had gotten separated from everyone after the lifts closed. With no one around to ask for help, he had skied from the top of the mountain and, in his words, " just kept skiing down."

And me? I was in a "high place" too. In years to come, this incident reminded me: *Don't react to circumstances without responding first with prayer.*

Simple Abundance

For of Him and through Him and to Him are all things, to whom be glory forever. Amen.

Romans 11:36 NKJV

I remember hearing of a Christian who was in great trouble, and who had tried every deliverance, but in vain, who said finally to another in a tone of the utmost despair, "Well, there is nothing left for me now but to trust the Lord."

"Alas!" exclaimed the friend in the greatest consternation, "is it possible it has come to that?"[12]

—From *The God of All Comfort*

THE ABOVE EXCERPT came from a chapter Hannah Smith titled "Much More Versus Much Less." As I read this chapter more than a hundred years after it was written, I could not help but think of the many books, news magazines, and television programs with the theme of simplifying our lives. All of these resources advise us to simplify our lives by getting rid of excess baggage. We should "*right*size" our lives—throw away the clutter in them, they say.

Hannah Smith said, "To come to the point of having nothing left to trust in but the Lord has, I am afraid, seemed to us at times a desperate condition of things. And yet, if our Lord is to be believed, His 'much mores' of grace are abundantly equal to the worst emergency that can befall us. The apostle tells us that God is able to do 'exceeding abundantly above all that we can ask or think.'"

What are the motivations behind simplifying our lives? A secular motivation might be to create more time for us to pursue the things of the world or to have more time to "get in touch with" ourselves. Who are we?

And a sacred motivation? If we were to apply the principles of Mrs. Smith's message—to concentrate on the "much mores" of our lives—I think we would truly find simple abundance.

What are some sacred "much mores" we can find or add to our lives? Spending time with a child—playing, reading, or mentoring. Volunteering to serve with a service organization such as Habitat for Humanity or the Peace Corps. Joining a Bible study—or teaching one!

My brother-in-law had a nursing-home ministry. Each week he held a worship service in the home's cafeteria. And each week his primary message began with this affirmation: "Your life is not over just because you are confined to a nursing home. You still have the opportunity to share the gospel and take others to heaven with you!" He was helping these dear saints see the sacred "much more" in their lives. Their hearts were lifted from the heaviness of their circumstances to realize that they still had abundance in life, the simple abundance of sharing their life with someone else. That little worship service started with seven and grew to fifty—half of the residents! My personal sacred "much mores" are motivated by the desire to invest in the lives of others. This is simple abundance for me. God's abundant grace manifests itself in many ways! What are your sacred "much mores"?

Do we really believe that God is able to do for us "exceedingly abundantly" above all that we can ask or think? First Corinthians 2:9 tells us, "Eye has not seen, nor ear heard, nor have entered into the heart of man the things which God has prepared for those who love Him."

We strive in the flesh to "make life simpler," just as Mrs. Smith's readers were striving in the flesh to "fix" their lives. If we simply rest in the grace of God that He gives abundantly through Christ, then even if temporal clutter or woes surround us, our focus will be on what truly matters, the "much more."

For when we were still without strength, in due time Christ died for the ungodly. For scarcely for a righteous man will one die; yet perhaps for a good man someone would even dare to die. But God demonstrates His own love toward us, in that while we were still sinners, Christ died for us. Much more then, having now been justified by His blood, we shall be saved from wrath through Him. For if when we were enemies we were reconciled to God through the death of His Son, much more, having been reconciled, we shall be saved by His life. And not only that, but we also rejoice in God through our Lord Jesus Christ, through whom we have now received the reconciliation.

Romans 5:6–11 NKJV

Timeless Moments

BY JONI EARECKSON TADA

"Be very careful, then, how you live—not as unwise but as wise, making the most of every opportunity, because the days are evil."

Ephesians 5:15-16 NIV

LAST EVENING as I left my office, I was struck by a glorious sunset, a sassy kaleidoscope of vivid lilac and bright pink. I faced the color, letting it wash me in its golden glow. But suddenly, just as the color was at its peak . . . it vanished.

As I got into my van, I remembered a thought by Amy Carmichael, "We will have all of eternity to celebrate the victories and only a few hours before sunset in which to win them."

Like a sunset, life will soon be over in a flash. All the color and glory that we now enjoy will one day suddenly vanish. When we stand on the other side of eternity, I wonder if we will be amazed that life went by so quickly. I suspect that at that time we literally will not have time to think about it.

That's why we must think about it presently and realize there are timeless moments to be lived right now. A smile for the gas station attendant. A pleasant "God bless you" for the woman at the market. A hug for your spouse, straight from the heart. Prayers offered in spirit and truth.

Amy Carmichael would call these victories—and there is little time to collect these, the small victories. The days are fleeting, the hours are evaporating. Before you know it, our chance to prove our love for Jesus will fade. The sun will have set. So hear the echo of Paul's words and make the most of every opportunity.

Dear Father, sometimes I live as though this life will go on forever. I realize that it will not, so help me today to live timeless moments for Jesus. Help me to win victories, no matter how small, for You.[13]

—From *Diamonds in the Dust*

VICTORY THROUGH EXAMPLE

We give thanks to God always for you all,
making mention of you in our prayers,
remembering without ceasing your work of faith,
labor of love, and patience of hope
in our Lord Jesus Christ in the sight
of our God and Father,
knowing, beloved brethren,
your election by God.

1 Thessalonians 1:2–4 NKJV

Sustaining Joy

Again, the kingdom of heaven is like treasure hidden in a field, which a man found and hid; and for joy over it he goes and sells all that he has and buys that field.

Matthew 13:44 NKJV

The highest joy to the Christian almost always comes through suffering. No flower can bloom in Paradise which is not transplanted from Gethsemane. No one can taste of the fruit of the tree of life, that has not tasted of the fruits of the tree of Calvary. The crown is after the cross.

To pursue joy is to lose it. The only way to get it is to follow steadily the path of duty, without thinking of joy, and then like sheep, it comes most surely unsought, and we "being in the way," the angel of God, bright-haired Joy, is sure to meet us.

—Alexander Maclauren (1826–1910), Scottish theologian

IF YOU ASKED people "What is joy?" you would probably get a variety of responses, including *well-being, contentment, happiness, rejoicing*, and *delight*.

When Christ told the Parable of the Hidden Treasure to describe the kingdom of heaven and then asked His listeners if they understood what he was saying, they answered yes.

When I looked at that passage, my first thought was, *Of course! They would say yes, because they were happy, content, and rejoicing that they were gazing and listening to Christ!* They had found the kingdom of heaven—Christ was their kingdom of heaven, and He was still with them.

What happened when Christ's physical presence was gone from their lives? They probably experienced denial, shock, pain, and anger. But after time, three days to be exact, Christ came back! Joy again! But then He told them He would be leaving them again.

Think back to the moment of your salvation. Remember how you felt? Oh, the joy! God was in heaven and Jesus was in your heart. All was right in the world. But before you knew it, the world began inching its way back into your life, trying to push Christ from it! Then before you knew it, the joy was gone.

At least you *thought* the joy was gone. But Christ, the hidden treasure, didn't leave, so where was the joy?

Sustaining joy—the joy that just keeps on keeping on—is always a part of us. Sustaining joy comes with daily living, spiritual maturing, and experience.

When Jesus told the disciples that He was going away, their hearts were so filled with sorrow that they didn't even ask where He was going. I wonder if it even registered when Jesus explained that the Holy Spirit was coming in His place.

Then some of His disciples said among themselves, "What is this that He says to us, 'A little while, and you will not see Me'; and . . . , 'because I go to the Father?'" They said therefore, "What is this that He says, 'A little while'? We do not know what He is saying." Now Jesus knew that they desired to ask Him, and He said to them, "Are you inquiring among yourselves about what I said, 'A little while, and you will not see Me; and again a little while, and you will see Me'? Most assuredly, I say to you that you will weep and lament, but the world will rejoice; and you will be sorrowful, but your sorrow will be turned into joy."

John 16:17–20 NKJV

Is this what Maclauren meant by "suffering to experience joy"? Certainly the disciples had no idea that they would be exiled from the synagogues and slain as martyrs, killed by men who thought they were doing God a service (John 16:1–2). No, I think they sustained joy by living each day for Christ and not for themselves. And, they steadily followed their "path of duty" and just by "being in the way" were met by that bright-haired angel, Joy.

Unsought, yet sustaining, joy comes through growing in the knowledge of God and living by that knowledge—in spite of our circumstances.

Resurrection: Jesus and the Saved

And let us not grow weary while doing good, for in due season we shall reap if we do not lose heart.

Galatians 6:9 NKJV

The records represent Christ . . . as withdrawing six weeks later, into some different mode of existence. It says—He says—that He goes "to prepare a place for us." This presumably means that He is about to create that whole new Nature which will provide the environment or conditions for His glorified humanity and, in Him, for ours . . . It is not the picture of an escape from any and every kind of Nature into some unconditioned and utterly transcendent life. It is the picture of a new human nature and a new Nature in general, being brought into existence . . . The old field of space, time, matter, and the senses is to be weeded, dug, and sown for a new crop. We may be tired of that old field: God is not.[14]

—From *The Quotable Lewis*

WHEN I READ Lewis' phrase "tired of that old field," I think of the Scripture, quoted above, that hangs on my closet door and greets me everyday.

As Christians, we have the duty of watchfulness. Second Timothy 4:5 reminds us, "But you be watchful in all things, endure afflictions, do the work of an evangelist, fulfill your ministry." We should always anticipate resurrection in our lives.

Have you ever grown weary of doing good? It can happen. Sometimes our physical and spiritual resources become depleted, and we wonder whether we can do one more thing.

At times like those, we must remember God's grace and fasten our hope on what is to come:

> But God, who is rich in mercy, . . .
> even when we were dead in trespasses, made us alive together with Christ (by grace you have been saved), and raised us up together . . .
> that in the ages to come He might show the exceeding riches of His grace in His kindnes toward us in Christ Jesus.
>
> Ephesians 1:4–6 NKJV

When I do this, I am refreshed, and my passion to stay within His will is renewed. My human nature may grow weary, but He who is within me does not!

The Source of Strength

Have you not known?

Have you not heard?

The everlasting God, the Lord,

The Creator of the ends of the earth,

Neither faints nor is weary.

His understanding is unsearchable.

He gives power to the weak,

And to those who have no might He increases strength.

Even the youths shall faint and be weary,

And the young men shall utterly fall,

But those who wait on the Lord

Shall renew their strength;

They shall mount up with wings like eagles,

They shall run and not be weary,

They shall walk and not faint.

Isaiah 40:28–31 NKJV

Seasons of Lives

BY KEN GIRE JR.

Jesus said to her, "I am the resurrection and the life. He who believes in Me, though he may die, he shall live."

John 11:25 NKJV

DEATH IS THE WAY of all flesh—a season to spring forth and flower, a season to fade and fall to the ground.

But if the seasons teach us anything, if they make one grand, eloquent statement at all, it is that death does not have the last word. True, the flower's petals fall to the ground. But so do its seeds. And though the seeds may sleep for a season under a blanket of snow, they will awaken in spring.

As they do, they lift their fragrant heads to hint of a springtime yet to come. Where flowers never die. Where the dew of tears never fall.

But the Elysian fields of paradise are far from the borders of Bethany. There, an untimely frost has settled over a friend. Lazarus is wilting fast. The news comes by way of a messenger.

"Lord, the one you love is sick."

Oddly, Jesus doesn't rush to his bedside. Not because He is too busy. Or because He doesn't care. But because the Father is orchestrating an incredible moment and needs time to set the stage. And since a corpse must be center stage

83

before this drama can begin, Jesus must wait until Lazarus dies before He can make His entrance.

But Mary and Martha can't see backstage in heaven. All they can see is an expansive, black curtain drawn across their lives. They sit at home, despondent, as in an empty theater, their tearful prayers returning to them like hollow echoes off indifferent walls.

It has been four days since their brother has died, but a mountain of grief still looms before them. It is a steep climb for the two sisters, and they feel they will never get over it. As Jesus approaches the outskirts of the city, a disillusioned Martha rushes out to greet Him.

"Lord, if you had been here, my brother would not have died."

Jesus meets her on the crumbling ledge of her grief. He steadies her with the assurance that He is in control.

"I am the resurrection and the life. He who believes in me will live, even though he dies."

The words provide a foothold for her. At Jesus' request, Martha goes to call her sister. Mary comes, her eyes puffy and bloodshot. The flood of emotions is still swift and turbid. She falls before the Lord like an earthenware vessel dropped to the ground, her heart shattered, her tears spilling over His feet.

"Lord, if you had been here, my brother would not have died."

Both sisters approached Jesus with the identical words. But whereas Martha said them to His face, Mary cried them at His feet. Maybe that is why the one evokes only a theological truth, while the other evokes His tears.

Twice the Scriptures blot the tears of our Lord. On a hill overlooking Jerusalem, as He weeps for the nation. And on the way to a friend's grave, as He weeps for those who grieve.

What an incredible Savior. Weeping not just *for* us in our sin but *with* us in our suffering. Stooping to share our yoke so the burden of grief may be lessened.

But how do the tears He shared with Mary fit with the theological truth He shared with Martha? Who can reconcile the words *Jesus wept* with *I am the resurrection and the life*?

So strange that one with such absolute power would surrender so quickly to so small an army as tears.

But He does.

And for a beautifully tender moment, we are given the privilege to glimpse one of the most provocative embraces between deity and humanity in all the Scriptures.

On our way to Lazarus' tomb, we stumble on still another question. Jesus approaches the gravesite with the full assurance that He will raise his friend from the dead. Why then does the sight of the tomb trouble Him?

Maybe the tomb in the garden is too graphic a reminder of Eden gone to seed. Of Paradise lost. And of the cold, dark tomb He would have to enter to regain it.

In any case, it is remarkable that *our* plight could trouble *His* spirit; that *our* pain could summon *His* tears.

The raising of Lazarus is the most daring and dramatic of all the Savior's healings. He courageously went into a den where hostility raged against Him to snatch a friend from the jaws of death.

It was an incredible moment.

It revealed that Jesus was who He said he was—the resurrection and the life. But it revealed something else.

The tears of God.

And who's to say which is more incredible—a man who raises the dead . . . or a God who weeps?[15]

—From *Moments with the Savior*

The Fullness of God

BY HANNAH WHITALL SMITH

Who is like You, O Lord, among the gods?

Who is like You, glorious in holiness,

Fearful in praises, doing wonders?

Exodus 15:11 NKJV

SPEAK TO HIM, thou, for He hears; and spirit with spirit may meet;

Closer is He than breathing and nearer than hands and feet.

Let us sum up, once more, the teaching of these five names of God. What is it they say to us?

Jehovah-jireh, i.e., "I am He who sees thy need, and therefore provides for it."

Jehovah-nissi, i.e., "I am thy captain, and thy banner, and He who will fight thy battles for thee."

Jehovah-shalom, i.e. "I am thy peace. I have made peace for thee, and My peace I give unto thee."

Jehovah-tsidkenu, i.e. "I am thy righteousness. In Me thou wilt find all thou needest of wisdom, and righteousness, and sanctification, and redemption."

Jehovah-shammah, i.e., "I am with thee. I am thy everpresent, all-environing God and Saviour. I will never leave thee nor forsake thee. Wherever thou goest, there I am, and there shall My hand hold thee, and My right hand lead thee."

All this is true, whether we know it and recognize it or not. We may never have dreamed that God was such a God as this, and we may have gone through our lives thus far starved, and weary, and wretched. But all the time we have been starving in the midst of plenty. The fullness of God's salvation has awaited our faith; and "abundance of grace and of the gift of righteousness" have awaited our receiving.

Would that I could believe that for some of my readers all this was ended, and that henceforth they would see that these all-embracing names of God leave no tiny corner of their need unsupplied. Then would they be able to testify with the prophet to all around them: "Behold, God is my salvation: for the Lord Jehovah is my strength and my song; he also is become my salvation. Therefore with joy shall we draw water out of the wells of salvation."[16]

—From *The God of All Comfort*

In this excerpt from *The God of All Comfort*, Hannah Smith gave us five examples of names of God. Did you know that the Old and New Testaments contain more than two hundred names, titles, and descriptions of God? There are more than one hundred fifty for Jesus, and the Holy Spirit has over thirty! I could list them here, but then you would miss the blessing of discovering for yourself who this God is who has saved you.

Here are a few of my personal favorite descriptions for God:

- God who gives endurance and encouragement
- God who relents from sending calamity
- God who is able to do immeasurably more than all we ask or imagine
- God the gardener (husbandman)

- God who forms the hearts of all
- God who sees me
- God, my confidence
- God who is compassionate and gracious
- God, the living Father
- God who raised Christ from the dead

Just a few! Yet, each name and description alone makes my life full! In Hannah Smith's words, "these all-embracing names of God leave no tiny corner of my need unsupplied."

Are you experiencing the fullness of God? He is there for every corner of your life. Look for Him. Recognize Him. Live in the fullness of your salvation!

A Golden Gate

Thus Solomon had all the furnishings made for the house of the LORD: the altar of gold, and the table of gold on which was the showbread; the lampstands of pure gold, five on the right side and five on the left in front of the inner sanctuary, with the flowers and the lamps and the wick-trimmers of gold; the basins, the trimmers, the bowls, the ladles, and the censers of pure gold; and the hinges of gold, both for the doors of the inner room (the Most Holy Place) and for the doors of the main hall of the temple.

1 Kings 7:48–50 NKJV

HOW GRAND Solomon's temple must have been! So much gold! How devastated the Jews must have been when it was destroyed. For them it was a place to meet God. Through gold-hinged doors they came into the presence of their Lord. But even Solomon in his prayer of dedication (1 Kings 8:27) knew that the Lord could not be confined within walls, that the temple was only in His name.

More than nine hundred years later, about 19 B.C., Herod started adding to the temple that had been rebuilt by Zerubbabel some five hundred years earlier. In Herod's temple plans, there were gates in the four walls surrounding his temple. Like Solomon, Herod used silver and gold on all the gates. Josephus, the historian, records that one gate stood out above the rest. It was called the "Beautiful Gate" because it was twice as large as the other gates and, unlike the other gates, was made of solid bronze. Christians have traditionally known it as the "Golden

Gate." The lame man met His Lord at that gate and was healed by Peter and John (Acts 3).

Today there is no temple. It was destroyed again seventy years after the death of Christ. But this does not mean that we are no longer able to meet God. There is one temple that will never be destroyed. Jesus said, "Destroy this temple, and in three days I will raise it up." The Jews replied, "It has taken forty-six years to build this temple, and will You raise it up in three days?" (John 2:19–20).

Jesus was speaking of His body as the temple and was referring to His death and resurrection. For the ancient Israelites, the temple was a place where they could have a relationship with God. But through Jesus' death and resurrection, we can now meet God anywhere. Praise God, the doors of our "Golden Gate" are always open! Will you meet your Lord at the gate?

> *"I am the door. If anyone enters by*
> *Me, he will be saved."*
>
> John 10:9 NKJV

> Nor is there salvation in any other,
> for there is no other name
> under heaven given among men
> by which we must be saved.
>
> Acts 4:12 NKJV

Our High Priest

Seeing then that we have a great High Priest who has passed through the heavens, Jesus the Son of God, let us hold fast our confession.

For we do not have a High Priest who cannot sympathize with our weaknesses, but was in all points tempted as we are, yet without sin.

Let us therefore come boldly to the throne of grace, that we may obtain mercy and find grace to help in time of need.

Hebrews 4:14–16 NKJV

The Call of God

BY OSWALD CHAMBERS

And I heard the voice of the Lord saying:
"Whom shall I send?"

Isaiah 6:8 NKJV

WHEN WE SPEAK of the call of God, we are apt to forget the most important feature, viz., the nature of the One who calls. There is the call of the sea, the call of the mountains, the call of the great ice barriers, but these calls are only heard by the few. The call is the expression of the nature from which it comes, and we can only record the call if the same nature is in us. The call of God is the expression of God's nature, not of our nature . . .

The call of God is not the echo of my nature; my affinities and personal temperament are not considered. As long as I consider my personal temperament and think about what I am fitted for, I shall never hear the call of God. But when I am brought into relationship with God, I am in the condition Isaiah was in. Isaiah's soul was so attuned to God by the tremendous crisis he had gone through that he recorded the call of God to his amazed soul. The majority of us have no ear for anything but ourselves, we cannot hear a thing God says. To be brought into the zone of the call of God is to be profoundly altered.[17]

—From *My Utmost for His Highest*

Calvary Love

For to this you were called, because Christ also suffered for us, leaving us an
example, that you should follow His steps:
"Who committed no sin,
Nor was deceit found in His mouth";
who when reviled, did not revile in return; when He suffered, He did not threaten, but
committed Himself to Him who judges righteously; who Himself bore our sins in His
own body on the tree, that we, having died to sins, might live for righteousness—by
whose stripes you were healed. For you were like sheep going astray, but have now
returned to the Shepherd and Overseer of your souls.

1 Peter 2:21–25 NKJV

If a sudden jar
can cause me to speak an impatient, unloving word,
then I know nothing of Calvary love.
For a cup brimful of sweet water cannot spill even one drop of bitter water,
however suddenly jolted.[18]

—by Amy Carmichael

EACH YEAR in our ladies' Bible study, no matter what we are studying, we always seem
to have a week or more when we take a close look at the words we speak. With some
trepidation and much conviction, most of us look back on conversations and find

ourselves guilty of *harsh words, idle words, gossip, groanings, complaining* . . . a long list. *Comfort, encouragement, love,* and *contentment* are on our short list.

What is "Calvary love"? Having a son and daughter just two years apart was the perfect mix for some healthy sibling rivalry as they were growing up. One day when my daughter was about six, I heard the usual commotion of a brother-sister tussle when my daughter yelled, "I hate you in my way, BUT I love you in God's way!" Well, she almost had it right.

My daughter understood that there was a way to love others—the way God wanted her to love—and in her little heart, she knew she would always love her brother that way. As she grew older, she learned—and prayerfully as we Christians grow older in our walk, we also learn—that real, Calvary love has no "our way."

Calvary love is totally without any conditions. We comfort unconditionally. We encourage unconditionally. We are content unconditionally. And we love unconditionally.

I have written in the margin of my Bible, in reference to 1 Peter 2:18–25: *Character is revealed by reactions.* I shouldn't have to turn to 1 Peter to be reminded of this. As Amy Carmichael expressed it, if I react with careless words, I know nothing of Calvary love, where Christ is our example.

The passage in 1 Peter speaks volumes to me. We usually react because we feel that our rights have been violated in some way. But this passage tells us that not only is Christ our example, but He is also the Overseer of our souls. When we react unrighteously, we are assuming rights we no longer have. When we accepted the Cross and all it represents—death to sin and resurrection with Christ—then our responsibility is to be like Christ and *to respond with His character in all things.* What goes into our hearts comes out on our lips. In all things, show Calvary love.

True Love

Though I speak with the tongues of men and of angels, but have not *Calvary* love, I have become sounding brass or a clanging cymbal.

And though I have the gift of prophecy, and understand all mysteries and all knowledge, and though I have all faith, so that I could remove mountains, but have not *Calvary* love, I am nothing.

And though I bestow all my goods to feed the poor, and though I give my body to be burned, but have not *Calvary* love, it profits me nothing.

1 Corinthians 13:1–3 NKJV, altered

Early Morning Mist

Jesus said to her, "Woman, why are you weeping? Whom are you seeking?" She, sup-
posing Him to be the gardener, said to Him, "Sir, if You have carried Him away, tell
me where You have laid Him, and I will take Him away." Jesus said to her, "Mary!"
She turned and said to Him, "Rabboni!" (which is to say, Teacher).

John 20:15–16 NKJV

IN THE EARLY morning mist she arises from her mat, takes her spices and aloes, and leaves her house, past the Gate of Gennath and up to the hillside. She anticipates a somber task. By now the body will be swollen. His face will be white. Death's odor will be pungent.

A gray sky gives way to gold as she walks up the narrow trail. As she rounds the final bend, she gasps. The rock in front of the grave is pushed back.

"Someone took the body." She runs to awaken Peter and John. They rush to see for themselves. She tries to keep up with them but can't.

Peter comes out of the tomb bewildered and John comes out believing, but Mary just sits in front of it weeping. The two men go home and leave her alone with her grief.

But something tells her she is not alone. Maybe she hears a noise. Maybe she hears a whisper. Or maybe she just hears her own heart tell her to take a look for herself.

Whatever the reason, she does. She stoops down, sticks her head into the hewn entrance, and waits for her eyes to adjust to the dark.

"Why are you crying?" She sees what looks to be a man, but he's white—radiantly white. He is one of two lights on either end of the vacant slab. Two candles blazing on an altar.

"Why are you crying?" An uncommon question to be asked in a cemetery. In fact, the question is rude. That is, unless the questioner knows something the questionee doesn't.

"They have taken my Lord away, and I don't know where they have put him."

She still calls him "my Lord." As far as she knows his lips were silent. As far as she knows, his corpse had been carted off by graverobbers. But in spite of it all, he is still her Lord.

Such devotion moves Jesus. It moves him closer to her. So close she hears him breathing. She turns and there he stands. She thinks he is the gardener.

Now, Jesus could have revealed himself at this point. He could have called for an angel to present him or a band to announce his presence. But he didn't.

"Why are you crying? Who is it you are looking for?"

He doesn't leave her wondering long, just long enough to remind us that he loves to surprise us. He waits for us to despair of human strength and then intervenes with heavenly. God waits for us to give up and then—surprise!

Has it been a while since you let God surprise you?[19]

—From *Six Hours One Friday*

SURPRISED BY GOD

When You did awesome things

for which we did not look,

You came down,

The mountains shook at your presence.

For since the beginning of the world

Men have not heard nor perceived by the ear,

Nor has the eye seen any God besides You,

Who acts for the one who waits for Him.

You meet him who rejoices and does righteousness,

Who remembers You in Your ways.

Isaiah 64:3–5 NKJV

The Thief

BY RUTH BELL GRAHAM

We receive the due reward of our deeds; but this Man has done nothing wrong." Then he said to Jesus, "Lord, remember me when You come into Your kingdom." And Jesus said to him, "Assuredly, I say to you, today you will be with Me in Paradise."

Luke 23:41–43 NKJV

He died—
the thief—
and yet,
before,
he'd cried
for mercy
and, what's more,
his tortured soul
had found relief.

He got
a death
that he deserved;
a Life
that he did not.[20]

—From *Clouds Are the Dust of His Feet*

105

Are You Ready?

But you, beloved, building yourselves up on your most holy faith, praying in the Holy Spirit, keep yourselves in the love of God, looking for the mercy of our Lord Jesus Christ unto eternal life. And on some have compassion, making a distinction; but others save with fear, pulling them out of the fire, hating even the garment defiled by the flesh.

Now to Him who is able to keep you from stumbling,

And to present you faultless

Before the presence of His glory with exceeding joy,

To God our Savior,

Who alone is wise,

Be glory and majesty,

Dominion and power,

Both now and forever

Amen.

Jude 20–25 NKJV

THIS PASSAGE in my Bible is under the heading "Maintain Your Life with God."

As we approach the twenty-first century, there is much speculation about the end of the age and the possibility that Christ's second coming is not far off. There was similar speculation about Christ's return in the fall of 1988.

Our daughter and her friend Lindsay had just entered junior high. Lindsay's dad said to her one day, "You know, Lindsay, some people think Jesus will be coming in just a few days." She exclaimed, "Now?! I just got to junior high, and I'm a cheerleader, and I think this boy I like likes me. He *can't* come now, when everything in my life is so good!"

How precious! What I love most about Lindsay's comment is what she didn't say. I think she knew that if Christ came she would be raptured with Him. Her heart was ready even if her human nature balked.

Are you ready? If Christ returns soon, do you know what awaits you?

I have given this a great deal of thought, as I think many of you have. I am confident that I am right with God. But the question that nags me is, Is this all that is required of me? My personal opinion is no.

God has been preparing us for Christ's return from the moment our faith began. For some the preparation has taken years; for others, only days. Nonetheless, since the moment we were saved, He has used many different methods to prepare us for our future: We have His Word; we have those who have been called to teach us; we have the evidence of His hand in our world in both wonderful and tragic events. We should be able to answer, "Yes, we are ready."

Our lives are a testimony to others, and many people may come to salvation because of what they see in our lives. But what about our friends and family who might not have taken that step of faith? Shouldn't we be doing more for them? If Jesus came and you were raptured today, you probably know some people who might be left behind. What will become of them? What can you do to pass the baton?

In *The Third Millennium,* Dr. Paul Meier said, "Pray as if everything depended on God while working as if everything depended on us."[21]

God is in control, and He knows who will be ready. We joyfully anticipate being delivered of the chaos around us. Our joy will be even more complete if we have also told our friends and family about the good news of Jesus Christ and salvation.

In this light, I am not ready. Are you?

My High Place

For my eyes have seen the King,
The LORD of hosts.

Isaiah 6:5 NKJV

All around her, in every direction, were the snowy peaks of the High Places. She could see that the bases of all these mountains were extremely precipitous and that higher up they were all clothed with forests, then the green slopes of the higher Alps and then the snow. Wherever she looked, the slopes at that season of the year were covered with pure white flowers through whose half-transparent petals the sun shone, turning them to burning whiteness.

In the heart of each flower was a crown of pure gold. These white-robed hosts scented the slopes of the High Places with a perfume sweeter than any she had ever breathed before. All had their faces and golden crowns turned down the mountains as if looking at the valleys, multitudes upon multitudes of them, which no man could number, like "a great cloud of witnesses," all stooping forward to watch what was going on in the world below. Wherever the King and his companion walked, these white-robed flowers bowed beneath their feet and rose again, buoyant and unsullied, but exuding a perfume richer and sweeter than before.

On the utmost pinnacle to which he led her was an altar of pure gold, flashing in the sun with such splendor that she could not look at it but had to turn her eyes away at once, though she did perceive that a fire burned on it and a cloud of smoke perfumed with incense rose from it.

Then the King told her to kneel and with a pair of golden tongs brought a piece of burning coal from off the altar. Touching her with it he said, "Lo! this hath touched thy lips; and thine iniquity is taken away, and thy sin purged" (Isa. 6:7).[22]

—From *Hinds' Feet on High Places*

DO YOU REMEMBER the first Christian fiction you ever read? *Hinds' Feet on High Places* was mine. Pat Brown, the woman who prayed with me at a Billy Graham crusade, sent it as a gift for my high-school graduation in 1966. I never saw Mrs. Brown after that life-changing prayer, but we wrote back and forth until my graduation.

In her letter enclosed with my book, Pat mentioned she had ordered the book from England. *Hinds' Feet* is a Christian classic today, but back then it wasn't so readily available. I was amazed that she had gone to so much trouble, but I am glad she did. This book in its allegory form had a profound impact on my life.

I think Pat Brown knew enough about me from my letters to know that my life was similar to that of Much-Afraid, the heroine in the book. Much-Afraid was a crippled, disfigured orphan brought up by her aunt, Mrs. Dismal Forebodings, her daughters, Gloomy and Spiteful, and their brother, Craven Fear. They were all members of a larger family called the Fearings who lived in a village called Much-Trembling in the Valley of Humiliation. Much-Afraid lived in a little white cottage and spent her days with wonderful coworkers, Mercy and Peace, in the service of the Chief Shepherd. As much as she loved working with the Shepherd, her life was still full of distress, not only because of her infirmities but also because her family didn't much like her working for the Shepherd. They came up with a plan for her to marry Craven Fear. This is when Much-Afraid escaped the Fearing family and journeyed with the Shepherd and new companions, Sorrow and Suffering, from the Valley of

Humiliation to the High Places, where she found a perfect love that casts out all fear. Her infirmities were healed when she drank and immersed herself in a great "river of water of life, clear as crystal" (Rev. 22:1). When she at last took a leap of faith with her straightened hinds' feet toward the outstretched hands of her Lord, He changed her name to Grace and Glory, and her companions' names to Joy and Peace.

This is a glorious picture of our journey toward victory and love beyond human comprehension. Much-Afraid's journey to final victory was not without pitfalls and depletion of strength, but she overcame!

What are the similarities between Much-Afraid and me? I may not have been physically crippled and scarred, but I suffered an emotional crippling. I finally discovered that we can choose to be victims or rise to the higher places that only God can offer us. We may have Sorrow and Suffering as companions on our journey, but at the end, we will find that our companions become Joy and Peace and that we are healed.

Uncommon Virtue: A Tribute

Do you not know that you are the temple of God and that the Spirit of God dwells in you? If anyone defiles the temple of God, God will destroy him. For the temple of God is holy, which temple you are.

1 Corinthians 3:16–17 NKJV

ON JANUARY 20, 1999, an unknown assailant shot and killed thirty-year-old Donald R. Block.

Don Block had been a coworker and friend for ten years. Many men and women considered Don their best friend. He had the uncommon virtue of giving everyone who knew him the gift of his total self.

I called him Donnie. We laughed often about the comment I made shortly after we met. I was giving advice, and I said, "Just consider this as advice from your mother. After all, I'm old enough to be your mother." He asked, "How old are you?" When I told him, he laughed and said, "Why, you're older than my mother!" So began our special relationship.

My husband said that Donnie didn't make friends—he built relationships. And during the last eighteen months of his life, Donnie built the most important relationship of all.

The dedication page of Donnie's Bible reads:

To my new brother in Christ (B. A. on 7/15/97), Don Block.

God bless you on your exciting journey through the rest of your life in the WOMB of ETERNITY!

Jay Zinn

1 Cor. 3:5–15

Don was working in Atlanta with us at his first Christian Booksellers Association convention when he met a new friend, Jay Zinn—a pastor, artist, and author. While Jay and Don were having lunch one day, Don prayed to receive Jesus as his Savior. Jay gave Don his own Bible with the special inscription noted above. When you read the passage from 1 Corinthians, you will know why Don came back from that lunch and said to my husband and me, "You bottled Christianity for me, and Jay capped it. Thank you."

Don pursued God with the passion he had for everything. He started attending church, made Christian friends, and asked us questions about God. He gained most of his knowledge about God from reading his Bible, which he always had with him. After his funeral, Don's ten-year-old niece told me that Don had said his Bible was his most precious possession. She asked if her Bible contained the same words as Uncle Don's Bible.

Don Block. How tragically and swiftly you were taken from us, but not before you started "bottling Christianity" in someone else's life.

BUILD ON THE RIGHT FOUNDATION

Who then is Paul, and who is Apollos, but ministers through whom you believed, as the Lord gave to each one? I planted, Apollos watered, but God gave the increase . . . For we are God's fellow workers; you are God's field, you are God's building. According to the grace of God which was given to me, as a wise master builder I have laid the foundation, and another builds on it. But let each one take heed how he builds on it. For no other foundation can anyone lay than that which is laid, which is Jesus Christ. Now if anyone builds on this foundation with gold, silver, precious stones, wood, hay, straw, each one's work will become clear; for the Day will declare it, because it will be revealed by fire; and the fire will test each one's work, of what sort it is. If anyone's work which he has built on it endures, he will receive a reward. If anyone's work is burned, he will suffer loss; but he himself will be saved, yet so as through fire.

1 Corinthians 3:5–15 NKJV

Footprints

The LORD shall preserve you from all evil;
He shall preserve your soul.
The LORD shall preserve your going out and your coming in
From this time forth, and even forevermore.

Psalm 121:7–8 NKJV

One night I had a dream—

I dreamed I was walking along the beach with the Lord, and across the sky flashed scenes from my life. For each scene I noticed two sets of footprints in the sand; one belonged to me and the other to the Lord.

When the last scene of my life flashed before me, I looked back at the footprints in the sand. I noticed that many times along the path of my life, there was only one set of footprints. I also noticed that it happened at the very lowest and saddest times in my life. This really bothered me, and I questioned the Lord about it.

"Lord, You said that once I decided to follow You, You would walk with me all the way, but I have noticed that during the most troublesome times in my life there is only one set of footprints. I don't understand why, in times when I needed You most, You should leave."

The Lord replied, "My precious, precious child, I love you and would never, never leave you during your times of trial and suffering. When you saw only one set of footprints, it was then that I carried you."

—Author unknown

Newness of Life

Now I saw a new heaven and a new earth, for the first heaven and the first earth had passed away. Also there was no more sea. Then I, John, saw the holy city, New Jerusalem, coming down out of heaven from God, prepared as a bride adorned for her husband. And I heard a loud voice from heaven saying, "Behold, the tabernacle of God is with men, and He will dwell with them, and they shall be His people. God Himself will be with them and be their God. And God will wipe away every tear from their eyes; there shall be no more death, nor sorrow, nor crying. There shall be no more pain, for the former things have passed away." Then He who sat on the throne said, "Behold, I make all things new." And He said to me, "Write, for these words are true and faithful."

Revelation 21:1–5 NKJV

WE HAVE LIVED in our home for twenty years. As constant as this house has been for us, so also has been its maintenance. A few years ago, for instance, we had to replace our roof. *So what?* you may be thinking. *What does this have to do with a new heaven and earth?*

Our contract with the roofers came with a forty-year guarantee! Forty years! How do they know the roof will last that long? I will be ninety-six years old when the warranty expires! All this is in writing, but the written contract will probably disappear or disintegrate before the roof does.

My point? I am amazed how much value we put on warranties and guarantees in our daily lives and how matter-of-fact we are sometimes in accepting God's written guarantee for our future. In light of eternity, forty years is insignificant. And nothing deteriorates in eternity. Once new, always new!

But we do not have to wait until eternity to walk in this newness of life. Christ's crucifixion and resurrection give us a whole new perspective on guarantees. Until Boo and I had our roof replaced, it was a constant effort to patch and cover the inevitable wear. Likewise, until our lives became new in Christ, we also struggled to patch the constant wear and tear on our lives. But the Holy Spirit, who never wears away, makes us brand-new.

Second chances are rare. Life usually doesn't rewind. Even a written guarantee is not a "sure thing." Except, of course, God's written guarantee. Think about it!

I was listening to a Christian radio station recently when the radio host quoted Charles Haddon Spurgeon. He said that Spurgeon once remarked that he wanted to die before Jesus came so he could experience the resurrection. What a glorious experience that will be! If Christ waits to return after we baby boomers are gone, then I will be rejoicing in the clouds with Spurgeon!

However, you must know that I also like to "seize each day" (*carpe diem*)! Living each day to its fullest gives a whole new meaning to this chapter on newness of life.

What am I to do with each day? Ecclesiastes 3 tells us that God set the yearning for eternity in the heart of man, yet some men mistakenly yearn for the temporary. They seize the day striving for the things of this earth. Newness of life means living a transformed life . . . *now!* Experiencing the JOY OF THE RESURRECTION . . . now! Eternity begins at salvation, and Jesus is on the throne . . . now!

Who is sitting on the throne of your life? Is your answer "I am" or "He is"? With one, the guarantees are only temporary. With the other, they are eternal.

As for man, his days are like
    grass;
As a flower of the field, so he
    flourishes.
For the wind passes over it, and
    it is gone.
And its place remembers it no
    more.
But *the mercy of the Lord is from*
    everlasting to everlasting
On those who fear Him,
And His righteousness to
    children's children,
To such as keep His covenant,
And to those who remember
    His commandments to do them.

Psalm 103:15–18 NKJV

Overcoming Obstacles

I will lift up my eyes to the hills—
From whence comes my help?
My help comes from the LORD,
Who made heaven and earth.

Psalm 121:1–2 NKJV

It has been well said that "early cares are a heavenly discipline." But they are even something better than discipline—they are God's chariots, sent to take the soul to its high places of triumph.

They do not look like chariots. They look instead like enemies, sufferings, trials, defeats, misunderstandings, disappointments, unkindnesses. They look like juggernaut cars of misery and wretchedness which are only waiting to roll over us and crush us into the earth. But could we see them as they really are, we should recognize them as chariots of triumph in which we may ride to those very heights of victory for which our souls have been longing and praying.[23]

—From *The Christian's Secret of a Happy Life*

DO YOU HAVE seemingly insurmountable obstacles? Look at them through God's eyes. Ask Him to open your eyes so that you can see Him lifting you above the "insurmountable."

Look at the people in the following list. They looked beyond the obstacles of their circumstances to overcome them:

John Bunyan (1628–1688)—Was locked in a prison cell. He became a prolific author; his most notable work was *The Pilgrim's Progress,* a great Christian allegory.

George Washington (1732–1799)—As commander of the Continental Army, he and his troops spent an entire winter in extremely harsh conditions (not enough food or shelter from the weather) in Valley Forge, Pennsylvania. Went on to become the first U.S. president and is one of the most important leaders in U.S. history.

Ludwig van Beethoven (1770–1827)—Was born to a drunkard father and unhappy mother. A master musician and composer, he composed many of his greatest works after he became deaf.

Sir Walter Scott (Scottish novelist and poet, 1771–1832)—Was crippled. His work as a translator, editor, biographer, and critic, together with his novels and poems, made him one of the most prominent figures in English romanticism.

Benjamin Disraeli (1804–1881)—Was subjected to bitter religious prejudice. Was a writer and served twice as prime minister of Britain. He had a profound influence on British politics for more than three decades.

Abraham Lincoln (1809–1865)—Was raised in abject poverty; his mother died when he was only ten. He and his wife had four sons; only one survived to maturity. Lincoln lost several elections before he finally became president. During his presidency, he faced the greatest internal crisis of any U.S. president—the Civil War. Lincoln is remembered for his vital role in preserving the union and for beginning the process that ended slavery.

Albert Einstein (1879–1955)—As a child, he was labeled a slow learner, retarded, and was written off as incapable of being educated. He went on to win the Nobel Prize in physics and was a true genius. Originated the theory of relativity.

Helen Keller (1880–1968)—At age eighteen months, Helen became deaf, blind, and mute due to scarlet fever. She grew up to become a highly intelligent, sensitive woman who wrote, spoke, and worked incessantly to help others with disabilities.

Franklin D. Roosevelt (1882–1945)—Though afflicted with infantile paralysis, he served longer than any other U.S. president. Roosevelt led the U.S. through two great crises—the Great Depression and World War II.

Joni Eareckson Tada (1950–)—At age seventeen, became a quadriplegic as the result of a diving accident. Overcame her disability to become an artist, a best-selling author, and a widely sought-after conference speaker. Founded JAF Ministries to accelerate Christian ministry to persons with disabilities.

Now, how about you? Are your obstacles really insurmountable? Why not pray about them? Keep in mind the following quote from Hannah Whitall Smith:

> *This is the prayer we need to pray for ourselves and one another:*
> *Lord, open our eyes that we may see,*
> *For all the world around us is full of God's horses and chariots,*
> *Waiting to carry us to places of glorious victory!*

Crystal River

And he showed me a pure river of water of life, clear as crystal, proceeding from the throne of God and of the Lamb.

Revelation 22:1 NKJV

HAVE YOU EVER wondered why standing by the edge of a river, wading in the ocean's tide, or listening to a babbling brook is so soothing? And the sound of a waterfall is indescribable!

My dream house would have two bedrooms on stilts! One side of each room would face mountains, and a second side the ocean. (The extra bedroom would be for guests.) There is such power in a mountain, strength that seems never to change. But the ocean has the power to change, and it can change your outlook on life. Do you think this is why so many vacations are spent by water's edge?

Water as a life-giving source is used symbolically throughout Scripture. For me the most profound passage is found in John 4 when a "woman of sin" finds Jesus at "the well."

A woman of Samaria came to draw water. Jesus said to her, "Give Me a drink." For His disciples had gone away into the city to buy food. Then the woman of Samaria said to Him, "How is it that You, being a Jew, ask a drink from me, a Samaritan woman?" For Jews have no dealings with Samaritans. Jesus answered and said to her, "If you knew the gift of God, and who it is who says to you, 'Give Me a drink,' you would have asked Him, and He would have given you living water." The woman said to Him, "Sir, You have nothing to draw with and the well is deep. Where then do You get that living water? Are You greater than our father Jacob, who gave us the well, and drank from it himself, as well as his sons and his livestock?" Jesus answered and said to her, "Whoever drinks of this water will thirst again, but whoever drinks of the water that I shall give him will never thirst. But the water that I shall give him will become in him a fountain of water springing up into everlasting life."

John 4:7–15 NKJV

Who could resist such an invitation? Sadly, some people do. When the Samaritan woman said she wanted to drink this water, she had to first confront her sin. Too many people today who hear this promise go away thirsty because they are unable to confront their sin. Their pain is too great and the cost is too high, or so they think.

One of my favorite pastimes at the beach is looking for seashells. (Isn't it everyone's?) Years ago I was walking early along a beach actually for exercise, not looking for seashells in particular. I was walking along at a fairly brisk pace and glanced down and saw one of my favorite shapes, a queen shell. This tiny shell has a smooth, straight edge at its base and a majestic fanned arch at the top. Preoccupied with ridding myself of cellulite, I didn't stop to pick it up. I thought surely I would see another one. But during that vacation and in the years since, I have searched and searched for that same shaped shell and have not found it!

Every time I set foot on any beach, I start looking for that shell, *the* shell. In my mind the queen shell has become a missed opportunity to find treasure. I didn't stop and pick it up when I had the chance, and I am the only one responsible for losing it.

The invitation to drink from the crystal river of life is also a rare and personal treasure. Sometimes people choose not to drink from the river because they don't want to confront their sins. Others procrastinate, thinking they will have another invitation, another time. But what if there is not another opportunity? What a tragedy it would be to spend eternity searching for what was once within reach!

It is impossible for me to conceive how anyone could stand at the water's edge and go away feeling lost—and choose to remain lost. The next time you see a river, ocean, waterfall, or brook, think of the Giver of this most wonderful gift.

And if you see a queen shell, stop, pick it up, and treasure it. Be reminded of God and His gift of the living water. Don't go away thirsty. Choose to drink from the fountain of life!

The First Dawn

Now after the Sabbath, as the first day of the week began to dawn, Mary Magdalene and the other Mary came to see the tomb.

Matthew 28:1 NKJV

THE FIRST DAY of the "rest of our lives" as Christians actually began with that first dawn of Christ's resurrection. Lamentations 3:23 says the Lord's mercies are new each morning. Without the mercy of Christ's resurrection, each new day would be merciless. I am so thankful that I can anticipate each day with the assurance that God will have yet another act of lovingkindness and mercy for me.

Yet, there are times when our days seem as bleak as Job's. Several years ago our family business was going through difficulty. Even though we had the assurance of God's mercies, some days seemed void of them. On one of those "Job" mornings, I awoke to the sight of my husband turning around and around in front of the mirror.

"What are you doing?" I asked.

"Checking for boils!" Boo exclaimed.

Do you have "Job" days? We all have days when our understanding is as lacking as Job's. Even when we question God, He continues to show His mercy rather condemning us for doubting Him. God spoke to Job out of a whirlwind and said, "Have you commanded the morning since your days began, and caused the dawn to know its place?" (Job 38:12).

I thank God for His command of that "first dawn" of Christ's resurrection, because now we can look forward to His mercies every day.

Notes

1. From *Keep a Quiet Heart,* 69–71. Copyright © 1995 by Elisabeth Elliot. Published by Servant Publications, Box 8617, Ann Arbor, MI 48107. Used with permission.

2. From *The Master's Indwelling* by Andrew Murray, 88–90. Copyright © 1985. Used by permission of the publisher, Whitaker House, 30 Hunt Valley Circle, New Kensington, PA 15068.

3. From *God Came Near* by Max Lucado, 38–39. Copyright © 1987 by Max Lucado and reprinted by permission of Multnomah Publishers, Inc.

4. From *Sitting by My Laughing Fire* by Ruth Bell Graham, 127. Copyright © 1977 Ruth Bell Graham (published by Word Publishing, Waco, TX). Used by permission of the author.

5. From *The Pursuit of God* by A. W. Tozer, 39. Copyright © 1982 by Christian Publications, Inc. Used with permission.

6. From *Gift from the Sea* by Anne Morrow Lindbergh, 37–38. Copyright © 1955, 1975, renewed by Anne Morrow Lindbergh. Reprinted by permission of Pantheon Books, a division of Random House, Inc.

7. "The Lighthouse" Copyright © 1998 Cord Courrege. Used by permission.

8. "Boundaries" Copyright © 1998 Cord Courrege. Used by permission.

9. From *31 Days of Praise*, 150–151. Copyright © 1994 by Warren and Ruth Myers, and reprinted by permission of Multnomah Publishers, Inc.

10. From *No Wonder They Call Him the Savior,* 163–164. Copyright © 1986 by Max Lucado and reprinted by permission of Multnomah Publishers, Inc.

11. From *The Holy Spirit of God* by Herbert Lockyer, 51. Copyright © 1981 by Herbert Lockyer. Used by permission.

12. From *The God of All Comfort* by Hannah Whitall Smith. First published circa 1875 in Mrs. Smith's husband's inspirational magazine.

13. Taken from *Diamonds in the Dust* by Joni Eareckson Tada, 366. Copyright © 1993 by Joni Eareckson Tada and used by permission of Zondervan Publishing House.

14. From *The Quotable Lewis: An Encyclopedic Selection of Quotes from the Complete Published Works of C. S. Lewis,* 515. Copyright © 1989, Wayne Martindale and Jerry Root, editors. Used by permission of Tyndale House Publishers, Inc. All rights reserved.

15. From *Moments with the Savior* by Ken Gire, Jr., 250–251. Copyright © 1998 by Ken Gire, Jr. Used by permission of Zondervan Publishing House.

16. From *The God of All Comfort* by Hannah Whitall Smith; first published circa 1875.

17. This material is taken from *My Utmost for His Highest* by Oswald Chambers, 16. Copyright © 1935 by Dodd Mead & Co., renewed Copyright © 1963 by the Oswald Chambers Publications Assn. Ltd., and used by permission of Discovery House Publishers, Box 3566, Grand Rapids, MI 49501. All rights reserved.

18. From *If* by Amy Carmichael, 46. Copyright © 1992. Used by permission of Christian Literature Crusade.

19. From *Six Hours One Friday,* 158–159. Copyright © 1989 by Max Lucado, and reprinted by permission of Multnomah Publishers, Inc.

20. From *Clouds Are the Dust of His Feet* by Ruth Bell Graham, 32. Copyright © 1992 Ruth Bell Graham and published by Crossway Books. Used by permission of Ruth Bell Graham.

21. From *The Third Millennium* by Paul Meier. Copyright © 1993 by Dr. Paul Meier, and reprinted by permission of Thomas Nelson, Inc.

22. From *Hinds' Feet on High Places* by Hannah Hurnard, 205–206. Copyright © 1975 by Tyndale House Publishers, Inc. Used by permission. All rights reserved.

23. From Chapter 19 of *The Christian's Secret of a Happy Life* by Hannah Whitall Smith. First published circa 1875.

About the Author

BEVERLY COURREGE and her husband of thirty years, Boo, have been involved in the Christian bookselling industry for twenty-five years. Many of the images in *The Joy of Resurrection* are available framed by Courrege Design and can be purchased at www.ChristianMarket.net along with Beverly's other books.

Their son, Cord, now twenty-five, is involved in the family's business, owns ChristianMarket.net and PageEngine Web solutions. Like Mom, with all this, he still finds time to write, and some of his work appears in *The Joy of Resurrection*.

Twenty-three-year-old daughter Jennifer (J. J.) works with a brokerage firm, where she met her fiancé. The whole family has become "wedding planners" and is looking forward to this joyous occasion in May 2000.

The Joy of Resurrection is Beverly's sixth book. She has a passion for God's Word which she desires to impart to her readers.

DAVID AND STEPHANIE EDMONSON use their gifts together to minister every day through photography. Many well-known speakers, authors, and Christian artists use the Edmonsons to help communicate what words cannot. David and Stephanie love to capture God's images in hopes of encouraging people in their understanding of God and their love for Him. If you would like to see more of the Edmonsons' photography, go to their Web site: www.davidedmonson.com.